333.95   Libal, Angela.
L694
          Rural teens and nature

Rural Teens and Nature
Conservation and Wildlife Rehabilitation

Title List

Getting Ready for the Fair: Crafts, Projects, and Prize-Winning Animals

Growing Up on a Farm: Responsibilities and Issues

Migrant Youth: Falling Between the Cracks

Rural Crime and Poverty: Violence, Drugs, and Other Issues

Rural Teens and Animal Raising: Large and Small Pets

Rural Teens and Nature: Conservation and Wildlife Rehabilitation

Rural Teens on the Move:
Cars, Motorcycles, and Off-Road Vehicles

Teen Life Among the Amish and Other Alternative Communities:
Choosing a Lifestyle

Teen Life on Reservations and in First Nation Communities:
Growing Up Native

Teen Minorities in Rural North America: Growing Up Different

Teens and Rural Education: Opportunities and Challenges

Teens and Rural Sports: Rodeos, Horses, Hunting, and Fishing

Teens Who Make a Difference in Rural Communities:
Youth Outreach Organizations and Community Action

Rural Teens and Nature
Conservation and Wildlife Rehabilitation

by Angela Libal

with Ida Walker

Mason Crest Publishers

Philadelphia

Mason Crest Publishers Inc.
370 Reed Road
Broomall, Pennsylvania 19008
(866) MCP-BOOK (toll free)
www.masoncrest.com

First printing
1 2 3 4 5 6 7 8 9 10
ISBN 978-1-4222-0011-7 (series)

Library of Congress Cataloging-in-Publication Data

Libal, Angela.
  Rural teens and nature : conservation and wildlife rehabilitation / by Angela Libal with Ida Walker.
      p. cm. — (Rural youth)
  Includes index.
  ISBN 978-1-4222-0023-0
  1. Rural youth—United States.   2. Teenagers and the environment—United States.   3. Conservation of natural resources—United States.   4. Wildlife rehabilitation—United States.   I. Walker, Ida.   II. Title.
HQ796.L434 2008
333.95'16—dc22
                                        2007010778

Cover and interior design by MK Bassett-Harvey.
Produced by Harding House Publishing Service, Inc.
www.hardinghousepages.com

Cover image design by Peter Spires Culotta.
Cover photography by iStock Photography (Alan Heartfield and
    Paige Falk).
Printed in Malaysia by Phoenix Press.

Contents

Introduction

by Celeste Carmichael

Results of a survey published by the Kellogg Foundation reveal that most people consider growing up in the country to be idyllic. And it's true that growing up in a rural environment does have real benefits. Research indicates that families in rural areas consistently have more traditional values, and communities are more closely knit. Rural youth spend more time than their urban counterparts in contact with agriculture and nature. Often youth are responsible for gardens and farm animals, and they benefit from both their sense of responsibility and their understanding of the natural world. Studies also indicate that rural youth are more engaged in their communities, working to improve society and local issues. And let us not forget the psychological and aesthetic benefits of living in a serene rural environment!

The advantages of rural living cannot be overlooked—but neither can the challenges. Statistics from around the country show that children in a rural environment face many of the same difficulties that are typically associated with children living in cities, and they fare worse than urban kids on several key indicators of positive youth development. For example, rural youth are more likely than their urban counterparts to use drugs and alcohol. Many of the problems facing rural youth are exacerbated by isolation, lack of jobs (for both parents and teens), and lack of support services for families in rural communities.

When most people hear the word "rural," they instantly think "farms." Actually, however, less than 12 percent of the population in rural areas make their livings through agriculture. Instead, service jobs are the top industry in rural North America. The lack of opportunities for higher paying jobs can trigger many problems: persistent poverty, lower educational standards, limited access to health care, inadequate housing, underemployment of teens, and lack of extracurricular possibilities. Additionally, the lack of—or in some cases surge of—diverse populations in rural communities presents its own set of challenges for youth and communities. All these concerns lead to the greatest threat to rural communities: the mass exodus of the post–high school population. Teens relocate for educational, recreational, and job opportunities, leaving their hometown indefinitely deficient in youth capital.

This series of books offers an in-depth examination of both the pleasures and challenges for rural youth. Understanding the realities is the first step to expanding the options for rural youth and increasing the likelihood of positive youth development.

CHAPTER 1
Life on Earth

Imagine living in a place where most of the trees and grass are primarily limited to small (very small) plots that break up a sea of concrete. Dogs, cats, and birds are the only animals to be seen, except in cages and habitats in zoos. Imagine that the only place you can get a fish for dinner is a grocery store or in a restaurant (already cooked).

For young adults living in a rural setting, that kind of environment might seem like something out of a horror story. Rural youth have the ability to walk out of their homes and into a sea of green—

trees, a variety of grasses, and other plants. Dogs, cats, and birds are common sights in the rural environment, but so are cows, moose, bears, horses, snakes, deer, rabbits, squirrels, and many other animals. And if a rural youth wants fish for dinner, there's often a pond near by stocked full of fish free for the catching.

Nature's *flora* and *fauna* are benefits of living in a rural setting. They also give rural youth a unique opportunity to see how human life interacts with the Earth's plant and animal life. This can also give them the opportunity to make a difference in maintaining the delicate balance between human life and that of nature.

A Delicate Balance

Planet Earth is a miraculous place, filled with the abundance of life. There is no known place on Earth without living things. From the fields and streams with which most human beings are familiar, to such inhospitable places as hot steam vents miles beneath the surface of the ocean, deserts, and the arctic and Antarctic polar caps— plants, animals, and other forms of life are everywhere.

Plants and animals are just two types of living things of concern to individuals interested in conservation. Scientists also study the *archaea* and *eubacteria*, *protozoans*, and fungi. The study of wildlife concentrates mainly on animals, as well as plants and fungi that support animal life. When protozoans and bacteria are examined in conservation studies, it is usually as disease-causing organisms, or as organisms that help sustain life, such as the bacteria in animals' digestive tracts that allow the digestion of food. All these tiny forms of life are part of Nature's web.

Living things do not exist alone, separate from one another. They are interwoven with their environments, the total sum of all living and nonliving things that exist in an area. Each individual element of an environment has a role to play in all other parts of the

In rural areas, people have the ability to come into contact with a variety of wildlife, including deer.

Planet Earth supports an amazing diversity of living organisms.

environment. If one thing changes, it affects every other living thing in that particular environment.

The natural conditions and environment where a plant or animal lives is called the habitat. A *localized* group of these living things and the environment they depend on is called an ecosystem.

Biodiversity

Each living thing on the planet has a special job to do in its environment. What these jobs are and how the organism does them has developed over millions of years in a process called evolution. One of the biggest influences on evolution is food. Plant and animal species naturally found in an area have developed the ability to thrive on the food that is available there. The food provides the nutrients the plants and animals need for survival, and animals have developed the ability to hunt for that food without undue harm to themselves.

The number of species in an ecosystem is referred to as biodiversity. Biodiversity is extremely important for the maintenance of life on Earth, both in the present and in the future. It is necessary for continuing life.

Biodiversity is crucial for sustaining present life because almost all species are dependent on other species to live. They depend on other species for food, for soil quality if they make their own food (such as plants' dependence on earthworms), for shelter, and even for bodily processes like digestion. The loss of a single species can often have drastic consequences for many species, beginning a chain reaction of destruction of the species dependent on it, and the species dependent on them. Life in an ecosystem is like a row of dominoes—knock one down, and it is only a matter of time before all of the others come tumbling down as well.

When you think about how dependent living things are on one another, it is easy to see how important each species may be. Consider, for example, that some animals (carnivores and omnivores) eat

An ecosystem is made up of a group of animals and the environment on which they depend. An egret is part of a wetlands ecosystem.

other animals, and how some of these animals (herbivores and omnivores) eat plants. Then consider how plants must reproduce. In order to make seeds, plants must be pollinated. While some are pollinated by the wind or are self-pollinators, most rely on insects and other animals, such as bats and birds, to carry the pollen between them. Honeybees are famous pollinators. Currently, the North American honeybee population is being killed off in huge numbers by a parasitic mite. Without the honeybees, many plants will not be **pollinated**. Without pollination, the plants cannot reproduce. This means there will not be enough food for the animals who feed on those plants and, in turn, too little food for the predators who feed

Rainforests of the Ocean

Ecosystems don't exist only on land. The ocean has a biodiversity all its own.

Covering only an estimated .2 percent of the area of the world's oceans, coral reefs provide habitat for a whopping 33 percent of all fish species. This does not include the countless invertebrates who rely on the reefs and who feed the fish, and the reef-building corals themselves. Coral are small invertebrate animals that secrete tubes made out of calcium and other minerals. The oceans contain both tropical coral reefs, such as those off the coasts of Central and South America, and deep-water reefs, such as those off the coast of Ireland.

Tropical coral reefs are the most studied. These reefs sustain an enormous diversity of life. They provide food, shelter, and spawning ("nursery") areas for most of the world's sea life. They are all extremely endangered by parasites and global warming, both of which threaten the available food supply for the animals and plants that depend on the reefs.

on those animals. This cascade effect is also bad for humans—many fruit farmers, not to mention beekeepers, are already feeling the destruction caused by this mite.

Extinction

Scientists estimate that between 3.6 and 100 million different species of living things are alive today. As of now, only about 1.8 million species are "known," which means they have been described by scientists. There remain vast tracts of habitat that have barely been explored, especially in the tropical rainforests and oceans of the world. Yet these areas are being so heavily exploited for human use that they are being destroyed too fast for natural processes to replace them (for example, by logging and by deep-sea trawling fishing methods). Due to the fact that human exploitation is moving faster than scientific study and conservation, species are being lost to extinction faster than they can be named and studied.

Extinction means that every last member of a species has died. A species that is extinct will never exist again. Every species and habitat that depended on the extinct species is also endangered by the dying out of a species.

Extinction has always been a part of the natural process of environmental change. Scientists say that in the past, the rate of extinction was about one species per million species per year. At the same time, new species arose about once per million species per year, so the total number of species on the planet remained roughly the same. Many species extinctions could be accounted for by evolution—where a species was replaced by its better-adapted descendants.

However, since the human population has expanded, species extinction rates have skyrocketed. The current rate of extinction is 100 to 1,000 species per million species per year. Scientists only know of

The Steps to Extinction

The International Union for Conservation of Nature and Natural Resources (IUCN) maintains the Red List of plants and animals that are extinct or are in danger of becoming endangered or extinct. When discussing the status of species, the IUCN uses the following categories:

- **Extinct:** the last remaining member of the species had died, or is presumed beyond reasonable doubt to have died.
- **Extinct in the wild:** captive individuals survive, but there is no free-living, natural population.
- **Critically endangered:** faces an extremely high risk of extinction in the immediate future.
- **Endangered:** faces a very high risk of extinction in the near future.
- **Vulnerable:** faces a high risk of extinction in the medium-term.
- **Least Concern:** no immediate threat to the survival of the species.

The last time there was such a massive wave of extinctions was when the dinosaurs vanished from the earth.

six other times since life first appeared on this planet when species have been lost in such numbers. The last time was the wave of extinctions that wiped the dinosaurs from the face of the Earth.

At the same time as species are being driven to premature extinction by human interference, new species are not arising in the numbers they once were. As habitats are destroyed and established species' genes are lost to extinction, the sources of new species and the ecosystems that would sustain them are being wiped out.

The world of ecosystems and biodiversity sounds complex. It might seem as though the efforts of one person, even a group of people, could not make much difference in the whole scheme of things. But, as has been described, everything is interconnected, and efforts to help one species of plant or animal can improve life on the entire planet.

CHAPTER 2
Conservation Efforts

Why do people move from the city to the country? Many times, the reason people offer is the desire to be closer to nature. Whether one lives on a working farm or just in a house in the country, nature's attraction is often a significant influence on where someone chooses to live.

But you can't live in the country (or anywhere else) without affecting your environment—including the water, land, animals, and other things found in nature. If care is not taken, in time, the very things that drew someone to a rural life will disappear, or at least be diminished. That's where conservation comes in.

21

Just by living on the earth humans have affected the lives of all other organisms. Some animals, like the dodo bird, have gone extinct as a result.

The Dodo.

294

Geo Edwards Sculp. AD. 1757.

What Does Conservation Mean?

Many people think that conservation means that people can't use something at all. That's not true. According to *Merriam-Webster's Collegiate Dictionary, Eleventh Edition,* to conserve means "to avoid wasteful or destructive use." A conservation program is one that provides "a careful preservation and protection of something." It does not mean, however, that things should remain the way they are. Nature is a living thing after all, so change should be expected. What needs to be controlled, however, is the effect of humans on nature.

The nature that surrounds us today is due in large part to the efforts of our ancestors—for better or worse. The fact that there are still many species of plants and animals alive today is the sign of a healthy environment. But the truth is that there used to be many more kinds of plants and animals. Over the years, however, some have become extinct because of natural and manmade causes. The Web site Earth Witness Community (www.earthwitness.com) has a list of more than four hundred plants that are believed to be extinct. Some *taxonomists* believe that some plants might have existed and become extinct even before anyone knew they were there.

Just as our ancestors affected the plant and animal life present today, so to will people living today affect the plant and animal life of the future. Over the past decades, the subject of conservation has aggressively come to the forefront of the public consciousness, including the attention of young people. Young people can do many things on their own to practice good conservation measures.

Becoming Conservation Aware

Youth who live in rural areas have a front seat to many of the conditions about which many conservationists have expressed serious concern. Urban kids might have to travel some distance to find a river or creek bed so they can participate in water-based conservation efforts—but, many farms and other rural properties have on them a creek or pond; rivers are also often nearby. City kids might have difficulty working with animal conservation; those living in rural areas have a vast array of animals available.

Regardless of whether one lives in an urban or rural area, it is important to first learn as much as possible about the subject of conservation. For rural students, 4-H groups are an important source of information. Both Boy Scouts and Girl Scouts have programs that deal with conservation and wildlife rehabilitation. The Sierra Club and county extension services can provide information about conservation programs and camps.

Each county in the United States has a county extension office full of information about conservation. The county extension agent is also available for information.

Types of Conservation

Nature covers a lot of areas, and each of them have conservation issues that individuals, regardless of whether they live in rural or urban areas, can become involved in. Not all of them require joining a group.

ENERGY CONSERVATION

The need to conserve energy, and change the source of that energy, has been talked about for decades. Still, problems exist, and more seem to rear their heads every year. For example, as the new millennium dawned, talk seemed to increase about global warming caused by the greenhouse effect.

Energy conservation is probably the easiest to practice. Youth can help their families weatherproof their homes, making them as energy efficient as possible. Other ways that individuals can help conserve energy is by:

- making sure doors and windows are closed when the air conditioner is on.

- setting the thermostat higher in summer and lower in winter.

- turning off lights when leaving a room.

- using energy efficient lightbulbs.

4-H

In the early twentieth century, people in different parts of the United States seemed to have the same idea. They wanted to help connect public school with living in the country.

But that wasn't the only reason people involved in agriculture looked toward young people. At the turn of the twentieth century, there were many agricultural innovations. Farmers and others involved in agriculture didn't jump on the bandwagon for these new techniques, much to the surprise of the U.S. Department of Agriculture (USDA). Though their parents and grandparents might not have been enthusiastic about the new discoveries, teachers found that young people were eager to test out the new innovations—if they had the chance.

In 1902, A. B. Graham helped a group of young people in Ohio have such an opportunity. Although it was not yet officially a 4-H club, the Ohio club is considered the birth of 4-H. In 1914, Congress created the Cooperative Extension Service under the USDA. The service created a club for boys and girls that became 4-H.

The four H's are: Head, Heart, Hands, and Health. Today's 4-H is international. Gone are the days of 4-H clubs separated by gender. Though raising animals, sewing, and making baked goods and jellies for fairs are still important, individuals involved in 4-H today tackle a variety of topics, including nature conservation.

Conserving energy can be as easy as turning off a light when leaving a room, or using energy-efficient lightbulbs.

What Is Global Warming?

Briefly, global warming refers to the increase in the earth's temperature caused largely by using greenhouse gasses—the burning of fossil fuels (such as oil and coal), land clearing, and agriculture.

Global warming results in seriously reduced glacier cover, which can make life difficult for such animals as polar bears; some scientists believe that extinction is a possibility for such animals. Higher sea levels and increased amounts of precipitation can also result.

Not everyone agrees that global warming is as serious as some experts predict, or that it exists at all. Still, the percentage of naysayers has decreased as evidence of global warming's existence and seriousness has increased.

• turning off the television, stereo, or radio when not listening to it.

• washing dishes by hand rather than in the dishwasher; running the dishwasher only when full.

• doing laundry in cold water.

The burning of fossil-based fuels is the major culprit in the spewing of greenhouse *emissions* into the atmosphere. An important way to lower these emissions is to reduce the amount one drives or uses gas-powered equipment. That can be difficult for someone living in a rural area. If possible, car pool or take the bus. Some schools have special buses that run later than usual so rural students can participate in after-school activities. If buying a car, check fuel efficiency ratings and consider purchasing a *hybrid*. Vehicles and farm equipment should be tuned-up regularly, so they run and burn fuel efficiently.

If mowing the lawn, reconsider whether it is really necessary to use a gas- or electric-powered lawnmower. Though it might not be glamorous and it does take more effort, a manual push mower is better for the environment and gives you more exercise—making your body run more efficiently too!

SOIL AND WATER CONSERVATION

Soil erosion is a big conservation problem. When dirt, sand, and other soil particles run into waterways, they become polluted. If the erosion is bad enough, plant and animal life that live in the water can be killed. Dirty water can become a breeding ground for bacteria and disease, making the water unusable.

Youth with creeks, rivers, or ponds on their property can plant and maintain grass and shrubs to help prevent erosion. If broken stone is available, ripraps can be built, protective foundations made from broken stones. Like shrubs and grass, these help keep the soil on the land and out of the water. It's also important that any drainage areas be kept clear to prevent flooding.

Some rural youth have wooded areas as part of their backyards. For them, walking the trails provides exercise, relaxation, and just plain fun. It also gives them the opportunity to maintain the trails and paths, keeping them clear and *unobtrusive*; trails should be safe

Using a manual push lawn mower is better for the environment and gives you extra exercise.

Hiking is a great way to get out and see nature. Hiking trails should be safe for the hikers, but disturb the natural habitat as little as possible.

A New Trend— Conservation Landscaping

Increasing numbers of people want to be environmentally aware and are turning to ways of making their homes and lawns more friendly to the environment. One of those ways is through conservation landscaping.

The process begins with soil quality. Landscapers analyze the soil and provide it with the minerals and nutrients it needs to be healthy. It is then covered with vegetation that will help keep the soil where it belongs and not in any waterways that might be located near the lawn. Earthworms and microorganisms such as bacteria are introduced into the lawn to reduce the occurrence of weeds and the perceived necessity of using fertilizers and pesticides to maintain a nice, healthy lawn.

for the hiker, but not disturb the surrounding natural habitats of the plants and animals that live in the woods.

If youth do not have waterways or woods on their property, they can still help to conserve soil and water. Many parks departments have volunteer opportunities available for teens and others interested in conservation. Even ordinary lawns can have erosion problems, especially where there is rain runoff. Youth can work with their parents to prevent soil erosion by planting shrubs or constructing ripraps. Though the soil wouldn't go directly into creeks or rivers, it can enter the drainage system, which eventually empties into a creek or river that empties into a large body of water.

Other ways both rural and urban young people can help conserve water include:

- turning off the water while brushing your teeth.

- taking an occasional bath instead of a shower (filling a bathtub takes less water than running a shower), or taking shorter showers.

- fixing any leaks or dripping faucets as soon as possible.

- washing dishes by hand rather than using the dishwasher, and running the dishwasher only when full (it saves energy too).

- using ice to cool a drink rather than letting the water run to get cold.

- watering the lawn only when absolutely necessary.

- running the washing machine only with a full load or, if the option exists on the machine, use the small load setting.

When summer days get excruciatingly hot, it's a lot of fun running through sprinklers and getting squirted with the garden hose. And if the lawn needs watering, you're solving two problems at once—getting cool and giving the grass a much-needed drink. But if the lawn doesn't need watering, the grass could be damaged from too much water, and though you're getting cooled off, a lot of water is being used. And you could be causing a soil erosion problem as well. Getting a pool, even a small inexpensive one, can help solve those problems.

Avoid watering your lawn unless it is absolutely necessary. Watering too much is bad for the grass, can increase soil erosion, and wastes water.

FORESTRY AND RANGE CONSERVATION

You don't need to live in the country, or have a huge forest in your rural backyard, to work to conserve forests and wide open ranges. Parks departments and other organizations welcome volunteers to help them keep track of the trees and plant life native to the forest and range. Erosion is a problem here as well, and planting native flora can help manage that issue. If youth do have such areas on their property, the same work can take place at home.

Whether in a park, national forest, or on private property, it is important to keep track of the health of the trees and plants living there. To monitor growth and health, censuses are periodically taken to evaluate the needs of the area, and help is generally appreciated for that project as well.

FISH AND WILDLIFE CONSERVATION

Many people move to rural areas so they can experience wildlife and fish. But keeping the experience alive takes work.

Many farms and rural properties have fish-containing ponds. Algae occur naturally in such environments, but sometimes it can overrun the pond. When that happens, algae is said to have "choked" the pond because the oxygen supply is depleted or at least severely compromised. Without oxygen, the fish will die. Rural youth (and their urban friends) can help monitor algae growth in farm and park ponds (with proper supervision of course). To help get rid of the problem algae, carp or catfish can be introduced into the pond. They are nature's algae controllers.

Some people who live in rural settings enjoy having ducks, geese, and other waterfowl around. Although these creatures are cute and fun to watch, they do bring their own set of issues. They can be noisy, their droppings and feathers can be messy, and ducks and

Too much algae in a pond reduces the oxygen supply of the water so much that fish can die.

Ducks and geese can be interesting additions to ponds, but they are also noisy and messy.

Water, Water Everywhere

"Water, water, every where,

Nor any drop to drink."

Those words are from the poem "The Rime of the Ancient Mariner" by Samuel Taylor Coleridge, but they might also be seen as a prophecy for today's world.

According to the World Health Organization, WHO, in 2004, more than one billion people did not have access to clean, safe drinking water. What most of us take for granted means life or death in many areas of the world, especially sub-Saharan Africa.

geese do like to nip. Before doing anything that will encourage waterfowl to visit a particular pond, make sure they'll be wanted! For ponds that welcome waterfowl, individuals can help make and place nesting boxes.

Young people can help plant trees in forests and wooded areas. Not only will the trees help prevent soil erosion as they mature, they will provide habitats for birds and animals.

Perhaps one of the most important ways to practice wildlife conservation is to not have wild animals as pets. Never purchase a pet that was captured in the wild. Even though exotic pets have become

Chipmunks and other wild animals may be cute, but they should not be caught and kept as pets.

more popular and some are now bred in captivity, there are many still caught in the wild to be sold as pets. And these aren't just baby alligators or similar types of animals. Chipmunks, ground squirrels, snakes, birds, and even deer are among those animals individuals have taken from the wild and tried to turn into pets.

It may seem like a harmless thing to do. After all, you'll be providing a safe and warm environment with plenty of food and water available. Unfortunately, someone's good intentions can cause more harm than good. First, this hurts wild ecosystems because it removes animals that fill important roles in the environment. Second, it hurts the animals themselves. If an animal must be caught in the wild in order to be kept as a pet, it is because there is not a captive population. And there's a good reason for that: if there is not a captive population, it is because the animal is difficult to keep alive in captivity. Also, for every wild animal that lives to reach a pet store, dozens more die in transit. The humane choice is to only adopt animals that have been bred in captivity.

Other Issues and Ways to Help

Conservation is not the only way young people—urban or rural—can help the environment. Like the conservation projects discussed previously, some of these can be done individually or in groups.

AIR AND WATER POLLUTION CONTROL

Air and water pollution is a major problem worldwide. Every individual has in his or her hands the power to make a difference in this area. Write state and national legislators encouraging them to give their support to legislation leading to strict clean air and clean water

Some people throw trash wherever they want. Those of us who care about the environment can help by picking up garbage others toss carelessly on the ground.

A Riddle

What do soda bottles, tables, benches, bicycle racks, cameras, backpacks, carpeting, shoes, and clothes have in common? They can all be produced with recycled plastic.

laws. Join efforts to plant trees along the highway; not only will they add beauty to the scene, they will reduce pollution coming from cars and other vehicles. At home and school, youth can help control air and water pollution by:

- using non-aerosol sprays.

- refraining from pouring pollutants into sink drains or drains on the street.

- quitting smoking—or not starting.

- using a bicycle or walking instead of driving or riding in a car.

- keeping motor vehicles running efficiently.

Common sense would say not to throw trash and other items into lakes, ponds, and other water sources, but people still do it. Not only do these things pollute the water, they can also be harmful to animals; for example, the plastic that holds six-packs of soda can become entangled around the necks of birds and waterfowl.

Recycling is one of the most important things you can do to help the environment.

RECYCLING

Recycling seems like such an easy thing to do, yet many people feel as though they "can't be bothered." And it does take an effort, but the effect on the environment can be significant.

Many communities require that trash be separated into garbage and recyclables. Glass, paper, certain types of cardboard, some plastics, and metal cans are collected into special bins and taken to be recycled into other products. Participating in such a program may be more difficult for rural youth, whose homes might not have a regular trash pickup. Still, many communities have drop-off centers for such items.

Heads Up About Paper Towels

Another way to help conserve natural resources and the environment is to buy items made from recycled products. Paper towels are among such items. It would be better for the environment to use cloth towels, but paper towels are very popular and are not going away anytime soon.

But be careful how you use paper towels made from recycled materials. Some contain traces of metals that, when the paper towel is used in the microwave, can cause a snap-crackle-pop—and possibly a fire.

A Land of Plenty

The United States is a land of plenty, and that includes waste. Tons of perfectly good food are thrown into the garbage each year. Instead, save leftovers for snacks or to take to school for lunch, freeze them to eat later, or combine them with leaves and grass clippings to make a compost heap to feed your garden. Disposable things like paper plates and cups and plastic cutlery are extremely convenient, but the environment pays a price. Though items like these can be recycled, others, like foam cups and dinnerware, take decades (if not longer) to decompose. Rethink their use. Is it really that important to save a little bit of time by using disposable dinner-ware rather than washing dishes? And remember, disposable does not mean throw anywhere. Dispose of properly, and pick up litter during walks in the countryside or at parks. Not only will the environment benefit, so will wildlife that can become injured by such products.

Youth are big consumers of soda. Whenever someone buys a soda (or other beverage) in a bottle or can, a deposit is paid on the container above the price of the drink. Once empty and rinsed out, the bottle or can is returned to the store or to a recycling center, and the deposit is paid to the consumer. Look for bottles and cans while walking, cycling, or riding in the car, and safely stop and pick them up. This is a painless way to earn some extra money!

But recycling doesn't have to be limited to bottles and cans. How many pieces of paper do you run through your computer printer? Once the original purpose of the printed page has been served, use the backs as scratch paper, or use them to print out other pages that won't have to be turned in for class.

Teens and other young people can make a major difference in the conservation of nature and the protection of the environment. But there's another area in which many individuals—including young people—can get involved: wildlife rehabilitation.

The Three R's

Reading, writing, and arithmetic have been called the "three R's" for almost as long as U.S. education has existed. But since the late 1980s, most North Americans have heard of a new set of "three R's": reduce, reuse, and recycle. These R's refer to ways to help the planet and its plants and animals.

Reduce the amount of resources used. This is as simple as limiting the use of things such as electricity and water, but also being careful what you buy and what you throw away. Purchasing items with less packaging creates less waste, as does using only what one needs.

Reuse means choosing items that can be used more than once. Passing on books and magazines, clothing, and toys, and choosing durable over disposable items are all methods of reusing resources.

Recycling is a very important way to manage our waste and conserve resources. Take advantage of community recycling programs. Recycling keeps non-biodegradable items like plastic, glass, and metal out of landfills, keeps toxic substances like plastic, oil, and some inks from being burned, and preserves our precious natural resources, like trees (recycling paper), petroleum (plastics), and metals (which must be mined from the earth).

CHAPTER 3
Helping Wildlife

Youth living in urban areas can go an entire lifetime without coming across a wild animal in need of help. Rural youth are much more likely to encounter an animal that might—or might not—be injured or abandoned.

What to Do if You Find an Orphaned or Injured Baby Animal

Often the best way we can help wild animals is by leaving them alone. These creatures evolved over millions of years, and are very specially formed to be able to care for themselves in a natural environment. The best way to help them is to allow them to live the way they are designed to live, free from human interference. Usually, they know what's good for them better than we do!

But sometimes individuals do come upon animals that need help, or at least seem to. Many times these are baby animals that appear abandoned. Most often, that is not the case. Generally, the parent is not far away and keeping a close eye on its offspring. When humans are babies, they spend a great deal of time with their parents. This is not true in much of the animal kingdom, where it is not unusual for young animals to spend time on their own.

People often assume that when they see a fawn on its own in the woods, it means the young deer's parent has been killed by a motor vehicle or hunter. This certainly does happen. But mother deer often leave their fawns alone while they go off to feed. Unlike other animals, fawns have no scent. This helps protect the baby from predators. It also means that the mother deer has no way to find her baby except to remember where she left it. The fawn is taught to stand still, right where it is left. If someone moves the fawn, the mother has no way of finding her baby, and a perfectly normal occurrence in nature has been thwarted by someone with good intentions but not so good knowledge of nature's ways. If the fawn is crying or still in the same location twelve to twenty-four hours later, then it needs help and a rehabilitator or game commissioner should be notified.

There are times, however, when hikers and others do come across orphaned or injured wildlife babies, and it is important to know what to do when they are found.

BIRDS

Young birds are some of the most often found baby animals. It is not unusual to find nestlings, baby birds that have yet to get their feathers, on the ground, usually right below the nest. This can happen for several reasons; a fall, a storm, or even a sibling spat can cause the baby bird to fall to the ground.

If the bird appears uninjured, it should be returned to the nest if at all possible. Contrary to popular belief, a mother bird will continue to care for her young after it is touched by a human. If the bird can't be returned to the nest, a replacement nest can be made using

Baby birds are often found on the ground, usually near their nest. This does not mean that they are abandoned.

Dogs, cats, and small children pose a threat to a fledgling on the ground. They should be kept away from the bird until it learns to fly.

If You Touch It . . .

How many times have you heard that if you touch a baby bird its parents won't care for it anymore? Well, it's not true. Generally, birds have a rather poor sense of smell. They won't be able to tell if you have touched their young.

a plastic container, such as one that contained spreadable margarine. Poke some holes in the bottom so water can drain out, line with paper towels, and tack to the tree near the original nest if possible. Then gently place the nestling into its new nest. Generally, the little bird's parents will return and feed the baby in its new home.

When baby birds become partially feathered, they are called fledglings. Finding one of them sitting on the ground needs to be handled differently from nestlings that have ended up outside the nest. Fledglings often jump out of their nests as part of learning to fly. Their parents will feed the young bird while it is on the ground, so no human intervention is needed, unless the bird is obviously injured.

Dogs, cats, and children pose some of the biggest danger to fledglings outside the nest. The young birds are usually able to fly within a few days, and in the meantime, dogs, cats, and children should be kept away.

If a young bird is injured or if it can be determined that it is really an orphan, there are things that an individual can do to help it.

According to the Web site *A Guide to Assisting Wildlife Babies* (www.tc.umn.edu/~devo0028/guideto.htm), finders of an injured or orphaned bird should:

- get it to a licensed wildlife rehabilitator as soon as possible.

- keep the baby bird warm and in a quiet, dark place until it can be brought in.

- do not give it any liquids (they will often inhale liquids).

RABBITS

As with all animals, rabbit parents try to keep their babies safe from predators. Their "nests" are generally small and located in grass, often under bushes. Mother rabbits line the nests with their fur and cover them with loose grass. Once the baby rabbits are born, mothers only come to the nest twice a day, once early in the morning and then again in early afternoon to feed their babies. This lessens the likelihood that other animals will follow her to the nest and kill the baby rabbits. The biggest threat to baby rabbits come when their nests are disturbed by humans or from cats and dogs.

By the time the rabbit is five inches long, it has left its mother and begun life on its own. Although it is still quite small, it is not truly a baby at that stage. Unless it's injured, it doesn't need human intervention.

Like fledglings, a baby rabbit found alone does not necessarily mean it is orphaned. If an uninjured baby rabbit is found outside the nest, it can usually be returned to the nest without a problem; the mother will still care for the baby after it has been touched by humans, but touch all of the babies so they smell the same. Because the mother only visits the nest twice a day, it can be hard to determine if she is still alive and feeding her young. If there's reason to believe she's not, place a stick or string, something that she would easily move, over the nest. If the stick or string is still in place the next day,

Rabbits leave the nest when they are still very small. Unless the rabbit seems injured, it should be left alone.

If a baby squirrel is found out of its nest, it is probably in need of help. If the mother appears to be absent, contact a trained rehabilitator for information and help.

or if the babies are cool to the touch and act as though they are hungry, the mother has probably been killed or abandoned the nest for another reason. The babies need to be taken to a wildlife rehabilitator as soon as possible.

Baby rabbits born in the wild do not adjust well to being raised by humans. Even under the care of specially trained rehabilitators or even veterinarians trained in their care, the death rate for such rabbits is extremely high, generally due to stress. Their survival depends on a special diet, antibiotics, and special care. Untrained individuals should not attempt to take care of these babies.

Should a baby rabbit need to be transported to a rehabilitator, it should be kept warm in a dark space. A small box with some towels in the bottom will work well.

SQUIRRELS

Unlike many other animals, if a baby squirrel is found on its own, it is probably in need of help. The squirrel may have fallen from its nest, or it may have adventured away from its nest because it's hungry. If one notices that the mother is absent for some time, it is likely that she has been killed.

If uncertain about the mother's status, the baby squirrel can be placed in a box at the bottom of the tree from where the baby likely fell to see if the mother returns. In the meantime, it's a good idea to contact a rehabilitator for information. She'll probably want the baby brought in. Like rabbits, the baby squirrel should be put in a warm, towel-lined box and kept in a quiet location.

RACCOONS, SKUNKS, AND FOXES

Baby raccoons, skunks, and foxes can often be seen in the woods. In most cases, they are simply playing, and their mothers are hiding, but keeping a careful eye on their young. As with other baby animals, it should not be immediately assumed that they need help,

In most cases fox kits should not be approached because the mother is probably hiding nearby.

Finding a Wildlife Rehabilitator

Begin by contacting veterinarians in the area. Even vets who specialize in small animal or companion animal care will probably have contact information for area rehabilitators. Don't expect vets to take care of wildlife, however. Such care is highly specialized, and most vets are not certified to provide such services. They can give you general information and help you find the right assistance.

Law enforcement agencies such as the police and sheriff departments and the game commission may also have contact information. Other sources include county extension services, university biology or animal health departments, or area veterinary schools.

You can also use the Internet to find a rehabilitator. The Web site www.tc.umn.edu/~devo0028/contact.htm provides a searchable directory of rehabilitators, as well as other search options.

Raccoons are frequent carriers of rabies. If raccoon babies need help, extreme caution should be used in handling them.

unless there is obvious injury or if they appear to be in a weakened condition or ill.

Should these babies need help, individuals should take extreme care in handling them. Raccoons, skunks, and foxes are frequent carriers of rabies. They should never be handled by anyone who is not wearing gloves. Contact a wildlife rehabilitator or the game commissioner for advice.

OPOSSUMS

Like rabbits, opossums become independent when they are still quite small. When their bodies are between eight and ten inches

Always Remember the Following:

1. A young animal's best chance for survival is to be raised by its natural mother. It is important to make every effort to try to return the young to its mother. Only after all efforts to reunite them have been exhausted should the orphan be removed from the wild. Do not try to raise the baby yourself.

2. All birds (except pigeons, starlings, and house sparrows) and most mammals are protected by law, and it is illegal to have them in your possession without proper permits from the federal and state government.

3. Proper care and nutrition are crucial to the survival of the baby, and any deficiency will more than likely cost the animal its life.

4. Baby animals easily imprint onto whoever is feeding them, and steps are needed to prevent this. An animal that is imprinted on people cannot be released back into the wild and usually must be destroyed.

Source: A Guide to Assisting Wildlife Babies (www.tc.umn.edu/~devo0028/guideto.htm).

Bears should never be approached except by an expert. Even the cute and cuddly looking cubs can be very dangerous.

long, they are on their own. Opossum babies smaller than that are generally found near their mother, who is often a victim of a vehicular hit-and-run accident. The babies need to be taken to a rehabilitator. In the meantime, they should be kept warm in a towel-lined box.

BAT PUPS

Bat pups are generally found after they've fallen from trees during storms or in buildings when they have ventured away from the rest of their colonies. When found, they need help and should be taken to a rehabilitator as soon as possible. Like raccoons, skunks, and foxes, they should never be picked up unless someone is wearing gloves, since bats often carry rabies.

BEAR CUBS

Who doesn't like a teddy bear? In the real world, bear cubs are another matter. As people have moved their homes further and further into the habitat once the domain of bears and other wildlife, the likelihood of running into a bear—adult or cub—has increased. And bears are dangerous, even the cute baby ones. Because of the danger presented by both the cub and its mother, this is a rescue best left to individuals such as game commissioners, who are experts in dealing with them.

What About Adult Wildlife?

Baby animals are not the only ones that might be in need of human assistance. However, when dealing with adult wildlife, special considerations need to be taken.

Though individuals can sometimes take baby animals to rehabilitators, it is usually not a good idea for adult animals to be handled

Do's and Don'ts of Transporting

DO:

- Place the animal in a secure cardboard box with small holes placed in the side or lid. The box should be just big enough for the animal to stand and turn around. Place paper towels or a soft cloth on the bottom of the box.

- Keep the box in a warm, quiet, dark place, away from family pets.

- If the animal is injured, cold, or featherless/hairless, put a heating pad on low under half of the box, with a folded towel in between the heating pad and the box. Small creatures that cannot move need to be checked to see that they do not get too hot.

- Try to get an animal help as soon as possible. Some birds need to eat every half hour. If you cannot get an animal help in 2 hours, call a rehabilitator.

by a non-professional. Most adult wildlife will do almost anything possible to avoid human contact. Should an adult approach a human, chances are good that the animal is infected with rabies. A rehabilitator or game commissioner should be contacted as soon as possible when this occurs, or if an injured animal falls into the cat-

DON'T:

- Keep peeking at the animal or handling the animal. The more you look at an animal or handle it, the more you stress the animal and reduce its chance of survival. Resist the temptation to put an animal inside your shirt. Cute little squirrels are notorious for being covered with fleas.

- Put green grass under an animal. It takes the heat out of them. Drying grass can be toxic to rabbits.

- Give any animal anything to eat or drink, especially cow's milk. Baby birds can't digest milk and many die. Many baby mammals are lactose intolerant and may develop diarrhea.

- Handle raccoons, skunks, fox, or bats.

Source: adapted from Wildlife Reference Sheet (www.tc.umn.edu/~devo0028/advice1.htm).

egory of those often carrying rabies. These include raccoons, skunks, foxes, and bats.

Individuals can sometimes transport injured adult animals to rehabilitation facilities, but great care should be practiced here as well—even if the animal does not show symptoms of rabies and is

An adult animal that approaches humans or acts strangely might have rabies. For example, a bat flying during the day should not be approached.

not one of the disease's common carriers. An injured animal is generally very frightened and may strike out at the person who is trying to provide help and comfort. It is not necessarily trying to hurt the person; the animal is frightened and doesn't understand that the person is just trying to help it. Even a small, frightened animal can cause a great deal of harm.

In general, it is best to contact a professional to get advice about how to best help adult wildlife.

Catching and Transporting

If an individual decides (with advice and instructions from a wildlife rehabilitator or game commissioner) to take an animal to a facility, there are specific ways to catch and handle it. These methods are designed to protect both humans and animals.

BIRDS

Generally, small birds can be picked up gently and placed in a paper bag with a paper towels inside and the top folded down. Larger and more active birds require different techniques. If someone is dealing with large birds with large talons, hawks for example, she should wear leather gloves. A sheet, towel, or box can be thrown over the bird to capture it. If using a box, slide a piece of cardboard under it so the bird stays in the box, and poke small holes in the top or side of the box. Nets should be used only with extreme caution, since they can hurt the bird's feathers.

Keep in mind that birds overheat quickly. Adult birds should not be kept wrapped in any kind of materials for a long time, as they will become too hot, which can cause them to die. Even holding an adult bird in one's hands can cause it to overheat after only a short period.

As much as you might want to help an orphaned animal, in most cases you should leave wildlife rescue to an expert.

MAMMALS

Baby rabbits should be picked up by hand and immediately placed in a box with small holes poked in the top. Experts recommend that all other baby mammals and all adult mammals should not be picked up with bare hands. Most can be caught by throwing a sheet or box over them. If using a sheet, it can be gathered after capture, tied, and used to transport the animal. As with birds, a piece of cardboard should be slid under a box used to capture an animal. Adult bats should be scooped into a plastic container or shoe box. Poke small holes into the lid, but keep in mind that bats can squeeze through holes as small as one-half inch!

A theme has run through this chapter: as much as someone wants to care for an abandoned or injured animal, it is usually best to leave such responsibilities to a wildlife rehabilitator!

CHAPTER 4
Wildlife Rehabilitation and Rehabilitators

According to *Merriam Webster's Collegiate Dictionary, Eleventh Edition,* "to rehabilitate" means to restore to former state. The Minnesota Wildlife Assistance Cooperative defines wildlife rehabilitation this way: "Wildlife rehabilitation involves caring for injured, ill and orphaned wild animals with the goal of releasing each into its natural habitat." Wildlife rehabilitation has its own 3 R's: rescue, rehabilitate, release. Wildlife rehabilitators are the individuals responsible for carrying out those goals.

13 Simple Things You Can Do to Avoid Harming Wildlife

1. <u>Prevent your pet cats and dogs from attacking and/or "playing" with wildlife</u>. Many injured animals are brought to the clinic each year with terrible wounds from dog and cat attacks.

2. <u>Alert birds to large expanses of glass in your home</u>. Hang streamers or place decals on patio doors or picture windows, or let them get a bit dirty to cut down on the reflection.

3. <u>Educate children to respect and care for all wild creatures and their habitat</u>. Children need to learn that wild animals are not toys and should be allowed to go about their lives undisturbed.

4. <u>Pick up litter and trash that could harm wildlife</u>. This includes six-pack connectors, fishing line, and batteries, especially watch batteries.

5. <u>Be alert while driving, especially near wildlife refuges and rural areas</u>. Animals do not know traffic safety rules, so they may dart in front of cars.

6. <u>As a general rule, leave infant wildlife alone</u>. They are not always orphaned. Be sure they are in need of help before you remove them from the nest area. If you find young birds on the ground, attempt to return them to the nest.

7. <u>Place caps over all chimneys and vents on your roof to prevent birds, ducks, and raccoons from taking up residence and becoming trapped.</u>

8. <u>Do not leave fishing line or fish hooks unattended or lying around outside.</u> Try to retrieve any kite string left on the ground or tangled in trees.

9. <u>Before mowing your lawn or tilling your garden, check for rabbits or ground-nesting birds that are in the way.</u> If you find any, consider waiting to mow or till. They won't be babies or nest-bound for very long.

10. <u>Check trees to make sure there are no active nests or residents of cavities before cutting them down.</u> Even better, avoid cutting down dead trees if they pose no safety hazard, since they provide homes for a wide variety of wildlife.

11. <u>Use non-toxic products on your lawn and garden.</u>

12. <u>Motor oil should not be left in oil pans unattended.</u> Birds often fall into these pans, and few survive.

13. <u>Do not attempt to raise or keep wildlife yourself.</u> Not only is it illegal, but wild creatures do not make good pets, and captivity poses a constant threat to them. Young wild animals raised without contact with their own species fail to develop survival skills and fear of humans, virtually eliminating their chances of survival in the wild.

Adapted from Wildlife Haven
members.tripod.com/~wildhaven/13simple.htm.

Although it sounds as though wildlife rehabilitation should be conflict-free, that's not the way it is. Some people believe that helping an injured or abandoned animal is contrary to nature. Illness or injury is nature's way of keeping itself in balance; the strongest will survive, the weak will not. Studies have shown, however, that most animals treated by rehabilitators were not injured or orphaned because of natural occurrences. Rather, humans and their actions caused events that led most of the animals into rehabilitation. Nature has no inborn way to deal with humans and the results of their actions.

It is the wildlife rehabilitator who comforts and treats the animals and prepares them to return to their natural habitat or, if they are unable to do so, gets them ready for life in a *sanctuary* or sometimes as educational resources in a zoo. If the injuries are too severe, it may also fall to the rehabilitator to humanely *euthanize* the animal to save it from suffering. It takes a special person to become a wildlife rehabilitator.

What It Takes to Be a Wildlife Rehabilitator

The decision to become a wildlife rehabilitator should not be made without doing a great deal of research. It is more than a job; it becomes a way of life and demands a huge commitment. According to the National Wildlife Rehabilitators Association (NWRA; www.nwrawildlife.org), rehabilitators need to be:

- self-motivated

- honest

- able to listen and speak well

Even if you are not a wildlife rehabilitator, you can do simple things to avoid harming wildlife. Driving carefully in areas where there are likely to be more animals is one way.

If a dead tree on your property poses no danger do not cut it, as dead trees provide homes for a variety of wildlife.

- willing to work

- cooperative

- energetic

- flexible

- a team player

- trainable

- positive

- eager to learn

- responsible

- pleasant

- able to acknowledge strengths and weaknesses

- confident

- tactful

- trustworthy

- concerned about wildlife, people, and the environment

Individuals who become wildlife rehabilitators must also be prepared to deal with highly stressful situations. The rehabilitator experiences successes, but she also must face issues surrounding suffering, death, and the very real danger that comes when working with sick and injured animals.

What Do Rehabilitators Do?

There is no hard and fast list of what rehabilitators do on a daily basis. It depends on what the types of animals they specialize in, where and for whom they work, and even the time of year (bat pups, for example, are often found in July and August). Some common tasks include:

- feeding baby birds or mammals (baby birds have to be fed up to fourteen times a day!)

- assisting with fluid therapy

- helping bandage and treat injuries

- supervising staff and volunteers

- providing public presentations about animals and the environment

- cleaning cages

- fund-raising

- capturing and transporting animals in need

- maintaining databases about animals

Most of the tasks are far from glamorous. But for someone dedicated to wildlife and wildlife rehabilitation, all of the tasks are well worth the good that he can do on behalf on animals and the environment.

Many of the tasks done by a wildlife rehabilitator are not glamorous. Feeding the animals and cleaning up after them are some common responsibilities.

Being a veterinarian is not a requirement for a wildlife rehabilitator. However, a biology or ecology degree is recommended.

A biology degree will provide the knowledge necessary for working with animals. Some colleges even offer wildlife rehabilitation course work.

Education and Training

Although some wildlife rehabilitators are veterinarians, veterinary technicians, and biologists, most are not. The NWRA recommends that most rehabilitators get a biology or ecology degree because it provides knowledge essential for quality hands-on animal care, develops an understanding of wildlife as they relate to humans and the environment, and gives one an edge in getting jobs; the field is becoming increasingly competitive.

More and more colleges are offering wildlife rehabilitation coursework within biology and ecology majors. Wildlife rehabilitation courses are often part of veterinary technician, veterinary assistant, and animal health education programs.

For those wanting to become veterinarians, many of the twenty-seven vet schools in the United States and four in Canada now offer coursework in wildlife rehabilitation. It is expected that a specialty or special certification in wildlife rehabilitation will eventually be offered within some veterinary programs.

Though it is not necessary to have a college degree to become a wildlife rehabilitator, it does require study and experience. If you live in an area with a rehabilitator or rehabilitation center, volunteer opportunities in working with wildlife are more than likely available. These opportunities can help you decide if this might be the right—or the wrong—career for you.

Wildlife rehabilitators also attend classes, seminars, and conferences to keep up to date on evolving techniques and theories in the field. They buy—and read—countless books and journals on the subject. They network with other rehabilitators and establish relationships with other animal-health professionals. Wildlife rehabilitators join professional associations. The NWRA suggests the following for individuals seeking a career in wildlife rehabilitation:

- Volunteer at an established facility or with an individual rehabilitator.

- Read and ask questions.

- Attend training sessions, conferences, and symposiums.

To become a wildlife rehabilitator, you will have to meet state requirements to obtain a permit and license. Rehabilitators who work with migratory birds and federally threatened and endangered wildlife must follow the rules and regulations established by the U.S. Fish and Wildlife Service and obtain a proper permit. States have their own regulations. It is illegal to have any protected animal in

Though it is not necessary to have a degree to become a wildlife rehabilitator, it is important to be educated.

your possession unless you have the proper permits. (If you're working with a licensed rehabilitator or in a licensed rehabilitation facility, it might not be necessary to have your own license.) In Canada, each province establishes its own licensing and regulation requirements. Requirements and licensing for rehabilitation of migratory birds falls under the domain of the Canadian Wildlife Service, Ministry of the Environment.

States establish any education or training requirements for becoming a wildlife rehabilitator. Some will require specific coursework and number of hands-on hours before achieving certification.

Where the Jobs Are

Wildlife rehabilitators are found in many places. However, the need for a wildlife rehabilitator would probably be greater where there is more of a chance for human–animal encounter.

Despite the benefits of working on their own, there is a major disadvantage for those wanting to be independent. In the United States, it is illegal to charge for animals that are brought to wildlife rehabilitators. The expense of being an independent wildlife rehabilitator can come as quite a shock. There's the cost of intake, transportation, food and medicine, boarding, and treatment that must be considered. Plus, there are books and journals to buy, conferences and symposiums to attend, special insurance policies to buy, and professional memberships to maintain. Being a wildlife rehabilitator can be very expensive. Many rehabilitators become nonprofit organizations, giving them tax options that can offset at least part of the expenses.

For those who choose to work for someone else, wildlife rehabilitation facilities can be a viable option. Wildlife rehabilitation facilities are generally located near high-population cities. Not unlike a veterinary hospital, these facilities have several types of jobs available. Employment opportunities also exist with city, county, and

Rescuing animals is an expensive pastime. Many rehabilitators become nonprofit organizations to help offset the expenses.

It is important to understand that death is a part of wildlife rehabilitation. Not every animal will survive.

state environmental education programs and with nonprofit organizations.

Volunteer Opportunities

For those too young for a career in wildlife rehabilitation or those who aren't sure it's the career for them, there are many volunteer opportunities in animal rehabilitation available. Many wildlife rehabilitators and wildlife rehabilitation facilities would welcome the help. (There are several other volunteer opportunities available besides those discussed here.)

BEST FRIENDS ANIMAL SANCTUARY

Located outside Kanab, Utah, Best Friends Animal Sanctuary is the largest sanctuary for abused and abandoned animals in the United States. Although most of the animals are cats, dogs, and horses, the sanctuary also houses wild birds, rabbits, horses, and pigs. It provides a safe home until an animal is adopted, or for the rest of the animal's life if it is not. Outreach programs help educate the public about animal care and responsibility.

4-H WILDLIFE CLUB

4-H Clubs sometimes get involved with wildlife rehabilitation. In Churchill County, Nevada, for example, the 4-H Wildlife Club has taken on the rehabilitation of baby barn owls as a major project. When area ranchers broke down their haystacks to feed the cattle, many baby barn owls were suddenly without a home. In 2005, more than fifty had to be placed with rehabilitators. The 4-H Wildlife Club decided to do something to reduce the number of baby barn owls in need of rehabilitation. They began the box-building project, creating alternative nesting sites for the owls. Members are notified when

Barn owls benefit from the help of the 4-H club in Churchill County, Nevada. The members build nest boxes and band owls to track their movements.

Green Chimneys

The animals are not always the only ones who benefit from rehabilitation. Sometimes the rehabilitators—especially the volunteer ones—are just as affected if not more so.

Green Chimneys offers residential and nonresidential programs for children with emotional, behavioral, social, and learning challenges. One of the techniques it uses is animal-assisted therapy. The success of horse-assisted therapy has long been proved. Though Green Chimneys offers horse-assisted therapy, it also operates Green Chimneys Farm & Wildlife Conservation Center in Brewster, New York. There students have the opportunity to help rehabilitate wildlife, as well as educate others about animals.

owls move into the new nests, and they band the owls so their movements can be tracked. They also help release owls that have been rehabilitated into areas where the box-nests have not been inhabited by other owls.

MONTEREY BAY AQUARIUM

In you live on the West Coast, the Monterey Bay Aquarium offers volunteer opportunities for individuals who want to help rehabilitate otters. Otters and seals are often the victims of oil spills.

Sea otters are often victims of oil spills. Volunteers spend hours cleaning the oil off the otters and making sure they are healthy enough to go home to the sea.

Countless volunteer hours are spent cleaning the animals and making certain they are healthy enough to return to the sea.

Though not for everyone, wildlife rehabilitation can be the perfect career for some lovers of animals and the environment. It takes a lot of work and can be emotionally taxing. For those willing and able to spend the time and money, people and animals will benefit.

The natural world is all around us, offering us its many gifts. There are many ways that each of us can help preserve those gifts. Every time someone appreciates the beauty and wonder of the natural world and makes a responsible choice, that person does her part to make the world a better place. There are many opportunities to do things every day that benefit the Earth and its creatures—and you don't need to be a scientist to do them!

Glossary

archaea: A group of bacteria-like organisms.

censuses: Official counting of populations.

emissions: Things that are produced or released.

eubacteria: True bacteria.

euthanize: To humanely put a living being to death.

fauna: Animal life.

flora: Plant life.

hybrid: Something made of a number of different elements.

localized: Limited to a specific area.

pollinated: Spread genetic material from plant to plant in particles called pollen.

protozoans: Tiny organisms, mostly microscopic and single-celled, that cannot be classified as plants, animals, or fungi, but are more complex than bacteria and archaea.

sanctuary: A safe place.

taxonomists: Scientists who study the classification of plants, animals, and microorganisms.

unobtrusive: To not be highly noticeable.

Further Reading

Ackerman, Diane. *The Rarest of the Rare: Vanishing Animals, Timeless Worlds*. New York: Vintage Books, Random House, Inc., 1997.

Adams, Douglas. *Last Chance to See!* New York: Ballantine Books, 1990.

American Zoo and Aquarium Association. *Species Survival Plans: Strategies for Wildlife Conservation*. Wheeling, W.V..: American Zoo and Aquarium Association, 1994.

Carter, W. Hodding. *Stolen Water: Saving the Everglades from its Friends, Foes, and Florida*. New York: Atria Books, 2004.

Fossey, Dian. *Gorillas in the Mist*. Boston, Mass.: Houghton Mifflin Company, 1983.

Goodall, Jane, and Marc Bekoff. *The Ten Trusts: What We Must Do to Care for the Animals We Love*. San Francisco, Calif.: Harper Collins, 2002.

Karesh, Dr. William B. *Appointment at the Ends of the World: Memoirs of a Wildlife Veterinarian*. New York: Warner Books, 1999.

Lentfer, Hank, and Carolyn Servid (eds.). *Arctic Refuge: A Circle of Testimony*. Minneapolis, Minn.: Milkweed Editions, 2001.

Robinson, Phillip T. *Life at the Zoo: Behind the Scenes with the Animal Doctors*. New York: Columbia University Press, 2004.

Thoreau, Henry David. *Walden and Other Writings*. New York: Barnes and Noble Books, Inc., 1993.

For More Information

Best Friends Animal Sanctuary
www.bestfriends.org

Boy Scouts
www.boyscouts.org

Earth Witness Community
www.earthwitness.com

4-H
www.4hUSA.org

International Union for Conservation and Natural Resources (IUCN)
iucn.org

Girl Scouts
www.girlscouts.org

Green Chimneys
www.greenchimneys.org

National Wildlife Rehabilitators Association
www.nwrawildlife.org

Sierra Club
www.sierraclub.org

Wildlife Haven
members.tripod.com/~wildhaven.htm

Wildlife Rescue and Rehabilitation
www.wildlife-rescue.org

Publisher's note:
The Web sites listed on this page were active at the time of publication. The publisher is not responsible for Web sites that have changed their addresses or discontinued operation since the date of publication. The publisher will review and update the Web-site list upon each reprint.

Bibliography

"Conservation Landscaping: A BayScapes Homeowner's Guide."
http://www.alliancechesbay.org/pubs/projects/deliverables-85-1-2003.pdf.

"Earth Day Stories." http://ww.wildlifehc.org/template.cfm?FrontID=4414.

Ford, Vikki. "4-H Wildlife Club Helps Save Barn Owls." Reno: University of
Nevada Cooperative Extension, 2006.

"4-H History." http://www.national4-headquarters.gov/about/4h_history.htm.

"New York State Wildlife Rehabilitation Council." http://www.nyswrc.org.

"The Principles of Leave No Trace Outdoor Adventures."
http://www.scouting.org/boyscouts/resources/21-105.

"Sierra Club Conservation Policies." http://www.sierraclub.org/policy/
conservation/wildlife.asp.

"Using Service Projects to Teach Middle School Youth About Environmental
Conservation." http://nationalserviceresources.org/epicenter/practices/index.php.

Index

Picture Credits

Fotolia.com
    Andrzej, Soja: p. 8
    Creswick, Brian: p. 29
    Farkas, Geza: p. 64
    Garris, Carey: p. 53
    Gelpi: p. 78
    Jokrdan, Michael: p. 77
    Lamping, Kevin: p. 35
    ljupco: p. 84
    ollirg: p. 50
    Pang, Tao: p. 54
    tboussac: p. 12
    Thomasi, Guido: p. 74
    Thompson, Cappi: p. 56
    Timple, Marti: p. 26
    Whitney, Aaron: p. 88
    Williams, Penny: p. 49
iStock.com
    Dominick, Sharon: p. 42
    Goodchild, Daniel: p. 68
    Loiseleux, Valerie: p. 66
    Picone, Paul: p. 14
Jupiter Images: pp. 11, 20, 22, 30, 33, 36, 38, 40, 46, 58, 60, 73, 79, 81, 83, 86

To the best knowledge of the publisher, all other images are in the public domain. If any image has been inadvertently uncredited, please notify Harding House Publishing Service, Vestal, New York 13850, so that rectification can be made for future printings.

Biographies

Authors
Angela Libal is the author of several books for young adults. She lives in California.

Ida Walker, the author of many nonfiction books, lives in New York State.

Series Consultant
Celeste J. Carmichael is a 4-H Youth Development Program Specialist at the Cornell University Cooperative Extension Administrative Unit in Ithaca, New York. She provides leadership to statewide 4-H Youth Development efforts including communications, curriculum, and conferences. She communicates the needs and impacts of the 4-H program to staff and decision makers, distributing information about issues related to youth and development, such as trends for rural youth.